Butterflies

Wendy Einstein
& Einstein Sisters

KidsWorld

What is a Butterfly?

Butterflies are insects. They have 6 legs and 2 pairs of wings. Some butterflies look like they have only 4 legs but they actually have 6. The front 2 legs are much shorter than the rest. They curl up, so they are hard to see.

Butterflies live on every continent except Antarctica. They can be found in all types of habitat, from cold Arctic tundra to hot dry deserts.

Butterflies are cold-blooded. That means their body temperature is the same as the air around them.

When they are cold, butterflies cannot fly. When you see them sunning themselves on flowers or leaves, they are letting the sun warm their bodies so they can fly.

Bodies

Butterflies don't have noses or lungs like we do. They breathe through small slits on their sides, call spiracles.

They have smell sensors on their antennae and taste sensors or their feet. So butterflies smell with their antennae and taste with their feet. Can you imagine tasting your food by standing on it? Better watch where you walk!

Butterfly bodies are covered with tiny scales. The scales are easiest to see on the wings.

Blue Morpho

Butterfly scales come off easily. If you touch a butterfly, some of the scales will come off on your finger. This doesn't hurt the butterfly and may actually save its life. If it gets caught in a spider web, the scales stick to the web but the butterfly can go free.

Some butterflies, like the blue morpho, have ears on their wings!

Eyes and Proboscis

Butterflies have compound eyes. Each eye is made up of many tiny eyes. Butterflies can see in all directions at once. But they can only see things that are close by.

A butterfly does not have a mouth, so it cannot eat food.

Instead it has a proboscis, a long tube that acts like a straw. The butterfly uses it to drink nectar from flowers or tree sap. The proboscis curls up under the butterfly's face when it is not being used.

Butterflies and moths
are closely related,
but there are a few
ways to tell them
apart.

Butterflies are usually
bigger. They also
usually have brighter
colours on their wings
than moths do.

Butterfly vs. Moth

Butterflies have long antennae that are rounded on the end. Moths have feathery antennae.

Moths are usually fuzzier.

Most butterflies are active during the day, though some are active at dawn and dusk. Most moths are active at night.

Families

Butterflies are grouped into
6 families: swallowtails,
brush-foots, whites and
sulphurs, gossamer-wings,
metalmarks and skippers.

Swallowtails are big butterflies. They are named for the shape of their hindwings, which look like a swallow's tail. A swallow is a type of bird.

Most species in this family live in the tropics. Some swallowtails, like the tiger swallowtail, live in southern Canada and the U.S.

Swallowtails

Brush-foots

Monarch

This family is named for the butterflies' 2 front legs. They are shorter than the rest and do not have feet. Instead they have little brush-like hairs. In some species the legs are so short that you can hardly see them.

The brush-footed butterfly family is the biggest group of butterflies. There are more than 5000 species in the world.

Mourning Cloak

Blue Morpho

Painted Lady

The family includes many of the most familiar butterflies, like the monarch, the mourning cloak, the blue morphos and the painted lady.

The butterflies cannot use their front legs for standing. They are used for tasting.

Whites and Sulphurs

Sulphur

Members of the whites and sulphurs group are medium-sized butterflies.

Most butterflies in this group are white or yellow. They may have black or orange markings.

White

The caterpillars of the whites eat plants from the mustard family, like cabbage or broccoli. Some species, like the cabbage white, are unpopular with farmers and gardeners. The hungry caterpillars can damage their plants.

The cabbage white was brought to North America from Europe in the 1800s. Today it is one of the most common butterflies in Canada and the U.S. If you have a garden, you've probably seen this butterfly.

Gossamer-wings

Copper

Gossamer-winged butterflies are some of the smallest butterflies. This group includes the hairstreaks, blues, coppers and harvesters.

Hairstreak

Blues, coppers and harvesters can be found in Canada and the U.S. Hairstreaks live in tropical habitats.

Many species of caterpillar in this group need ants to survive. The caterpillar's body oozes a sugary liquid to make the ants come to it. The ants protect them from predators.

Blue

The caterpillars of some species are carnivores. They eat other insects, like aphids or ants. Yup, that's right. The ant-eating caterpillars will snack on the same ants that protect them.

Harvester

The harvester is the only carnivorous caterpillar in North America.

Metalmarks

Most butterflies in the metalmark family live in tropical rain forests.

Some species that live in colder climates. The Mormon metalmark lives in Canada and the United States.

Metalmarks are named for the metallic-looking spots on their wings.

You can tell a male metalmark from a female by its front legs (if you can get close enough!). The males front legs are much shorter than its other 4 legs.

Skippers

Skippers have sturdy-looking bodies. They look more like moths than butterflies.

Most skippers are grey or brown.

Their antennae are also different than those of other butterflies. They are hooked on the end instead of rounded.

These little butterflies are pushy for their size. They are happy to push bigger butterflies out of the way to get to the flowers they want. They will even take on bumblebees and hummingbirds!

Most butterflies hold their wings open or closed as they drink nectar. Skippers usually hold their wings half open.

The Biggest

The biggest butterfly in the world is the Queen Alexandra's birdwing. It has a wingspan of about 10 inches (25 cm). That's as big as a dinner plate!

This butterfly is found only in a small area of Papua New Guinea.

The biggest butterfly in Canada
and the U.S. is the giant swallowtail.
It has a wingspan of about 4 inches
(10 cm), about as wide as
a coffee cup. It is found in
southeastern Ontario
and much of the US.

Giant
swallowtails
love citrus plants,
like orange and
grapefruit.

The Fastest Flyers

Many butterflies are a tasty snack for other creatures, so they need to fly fast to stay safe.

The fastest butterflies in the world are the skippers. They can fly 3 to 5 times faster than other butterflies.

Skippers can fly faster than a car driving on a city street.

Poisonous butterflies
do not fly as fast as those
that are not poisonous. They
are not as worried about
being eaten.

Temperature Extremes

Most butterflies like warm habitats with lots of flowers. But some butterflies live in extreme climates.

Some species of coppers, blues and sulphurs can be found in the Arctic.

Butterflies in colder climates are usually darker than their tropical cousins. This helps them absorb more heat from the sun.

Other butterflies,
like the desert black
swallowtail, live in
hot, dry deserts.

Life Cycle

A butterfly's life cycle has 4 stages. The butterfly looks completely different during each stage.

The first stage is the egg. Female butterflies lay their eggs on the plants the larvae (caterpillars) will eat when they hatch. The eggs are stuck to leaves or stems with a special "glue."

The next stage is the caterpillar stage. The caterpillar is an eating machine. It eats the egg sac it came out of and then the leaves around it.

As the caterpillar grows, it gets too big for its skin and must shed it. A caterpillar will shed its skin 4 or 5 times before it is fully grown. Each skin is called an instar.

Metamorphosis

The **third** life stage **of** a butterfly is the **pupa** or **chrysalis** stage. When the caterpillar has finished growing, it attaches its body to a branch or stem. It sheds its skin **again** and changes into a chrysalis.

A chrysalis is hard on the outside and keeps the caterpillar safe. Most chrysalises are brown or green so they blend in with the plant. Many creatures will eat a chrysalis if they find it.

The last stage is the imago stage. Tucked safely inside the chrysalis, the caterpillar changes into a butterfly. This change is called metamorphosis.

The butterfly cannot fly when it first climbs out of the chrysalis. Its body pumps blood into the wings so they spread out. Then the butterfly waits for the wings to dry so it can fly away.

Young and Old

Ever wonder what your favorite butterfly looks like as a caterpillar?

Monarch

Tiger Swallowtail

Cabbage
White

Lifespan

The time it takes for a butterfly to go from an egg
to an adult butterfly is different for every species.
Some can take 1 month. Others can take
a year or more.

For most species, the first 3 stages
take the longest. Most adult butterflies
live for only a few weeks.
Some die after only a few days.

The **mourning cloak butterfly has** one of the longest lifespans. It can **live** for about 9 months.

Monarchs **that are born in late summer** can live up to 9 months. Monarchs **born earlier** in summer live only about 1 month.

A butterfly's diet is more than just nectar and sap. Butterflies also drink juice from ripe or rotting fruit. They seem to especially like oranges and mushy bananas.

What Do They Eat?

Male butterflies will gather in big groups to drink from mud puddles or on lakeshores. They get minerals from the mud that they can't get from flowers or fruit. This behavior is called mud-puddling.

This is where things get a little gross. Male butterflies also mud-puddle on piles of poo, puddles of pee and rotting animal flesh. Who knew butterflies had such a dark side?

Butterflies also land on other creatures to drink their sweat or tears. Scientists think the butterflies like the salt.

What Eats Them?

Birds are butterflies' top predator. Many types of birds, like jays, flycatchers, robins and grosbeaks eat butterflies or caterpillars. The black-headed grosbeak is one of the few creatures that can eat monarchs, which are poisonous.

Frogs, toads and many types of reptiles, like lizards and snakes, are dangerous to butterflies, too.

Butterflies are not safe from other types of insects, either. Praying mantises, dragonflies, wasps, hornets and ants consider them food.

They also have to watch out for many types of mammals. Some bats, mice, rats, skunks and monkeys eat butterflies. The pygmy marmoset bites holes in trees so sap runs out and then eats the butterflies that come for the sap.

Staying Safe

Monarch

Many butterflies are brightly colored to warn predators that they taste bad or are poisonous.

Some butterflies that are not poisonous look like other species that are. The viceroy is not poisonous but looks almost exactly like the monarch. Because most predators stay away from the monarch, they also stay away from the viceroy.

Viceroy

Giant Owl Butterfly

Fake eyespots on their wings also help keep some butterflies safe. When a predator gets too close, the butterfly flashes its wings to show off the eyespots. This scares the predator away.

Predators often attack butterflies from behind. Eyespots on a butterfly's hindwings make a predator think the back end is actually the head. Then the predator attacks from in front of the butterfly instead of behind. This way, the butterfly can see the danger coming and escape.

Camouflage

One of a butterfly's best defenses is camouflage. Many butterflies have patterns or colors that blend into the background when they land to drink or rest.

Mimicry is another good defense. Some butterflies **look like other objects,** like a leaf or a flower.

Some species are brightly colored on the top of their wings but dull underneath. When they close their wings, they seem to disappear.

Escape!

Butterflies have a fluttering style of flying. Instead of going in a straight line, they fly up and down like a roller-coaster. Seems like a bad way to fly when trying to escape a predator, right? Not so.

The fluttering helps keep the butterfly safe because it is confusing to follow. A bird trying to catch a butterfly doesn't know where it will go next.

Brightly colored butterflies are easy for predators to see. But their flashy wings also help them stay safe.

As the butterfly flaps its wings, the brightly colored side is hidden for a second and then reappears. It looks like the butterfly disappears for a second and then reappears somewhere else. This confuses predators.

Caterpillar Defenses

Caterpillars also have to protect themselves. They can't fly away from danger. So what can they do to stay safe?

Some caterpillars have spikes or stiff hair that make them hard to eat.

Others ooze a nasty liquid so they taste bad. They can also give off a rotten odor so they smell bad.

Some caterpillars have huge eyespots. This makes them look like a bigger, scarier animal, like a snake.

Some caterpillars roll into a ball and drop off the leaf or branch to the ground when they are in danger.

Butterflies in Winter

Ever notice that you don't see butterflies in winter? So where do they go?

Many butterflies die before winter comes. Once they mate and the female lays her eggs, the adult butterflies reach the end of their lifespan.

A few butterflies, like the mourning cloak, live through winter. They hide under, loose bark or in holes where snow and wind won't touch them. That's why they are the first butterflies you see in spring.

Some species spend the winter as caterpillars. They find a safe hiding spot and go into a type of hibernation, called diapause. In diapause they stop growing. In spring they go into the chrysalis and turn into butterflies.

Other species spend winter in the egg or chrysalis stage.

A few butterflies, like the monarch, migrate in fall. They fly south to warmer places.

Monarchs are famous for their long migration.

There are 2 main populations of monarchs. One lives west of the Rocky Mountains. The other lives east of the Rocky Mountains.

Migration

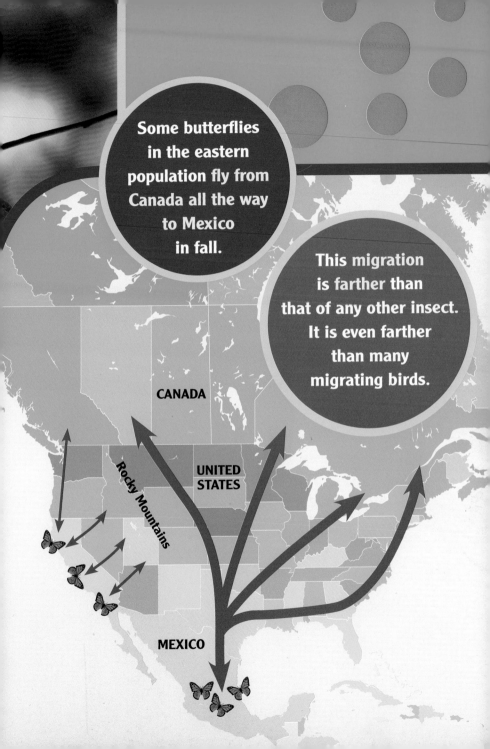

Heading South

Monarch caterpillars turn into butterflies at different times through the summer. Butterflies born in early or mid-summer live only a few weeks. The last group, born in late summer, lives up to 9 months. These are the butterflies that migrate south.

It can take the monarchs up to 2 months to make their journey. They must stop many times along the way to rest and drink.

Monarchs can fly only in daylight. At night they huddle together on plants to keep warm.

In Mexico, all the migrating monarchs go to the same oyamel fir forest, about an hour away from Mexico City. The forest is soon home to millions of butterflies. Each tree can have thousands of monarchs.

Northward Bound

The butterflies that make the trip north are not the same ones that migrated south.

These monarchs hatched from eggs laid by the females that flew south.

Nobody knows for sure how the new butterflies find their way to their northern habitat. Scientists think they use the sun as a guide.

The butterflies that leave Mexico do not make it all the way north. They fly as far as they can, then lay their eggs and die.

When the monarchs from those eggs are ready, they fly as far as they can. Then they lay eggs and die. It can take up to 4 generations before the monarchs reach their northern habitat.

Painted Lady

Monarchs are not the only butterflies that migrate. Painted ladies also migrate, but not every year.

Threats

Butterflies are an important part of nature. They pollinate many of the plants that other creatures rely on.

Some species of butterflies are in trouble. There are not as many as there used to be.

Habitat loss is the biggest threat to butterflies. People cut down the plants they need for food.

Climate change is also hurting some butterflies. They cannot survive big changes in temperature or the amount of rain in their habitat.

Pesticides also kill off many butterflies.

Conservation

Scientists watch butterflies and write down or take pictures of their behavior. If we understand how butterflies live, we can think of ways to help them.

Another way people are trying to protect butterflies is by putting a tiny tag on one of the butterflies' legs.

The tag lets scientists can see where the butterflies go and what plants they need.

One of the best ways to protect butterflies is to protect the plants they need to survive. Many projects today are helping keep the butterflies' habitat safe.

What You Can Do

If you want to help butterflies, plant a butterfly garden.

The garden should be sunny and protected from the wind.

Your butterfly garden should have some flowering plants from early spring to late fall, so plant many kinds of flowers with different blooming times.

The garden should also have some big, flat rocks so the butterflies can sun themselves.

Don't use pesticides or herbicides on your garden or lawn.

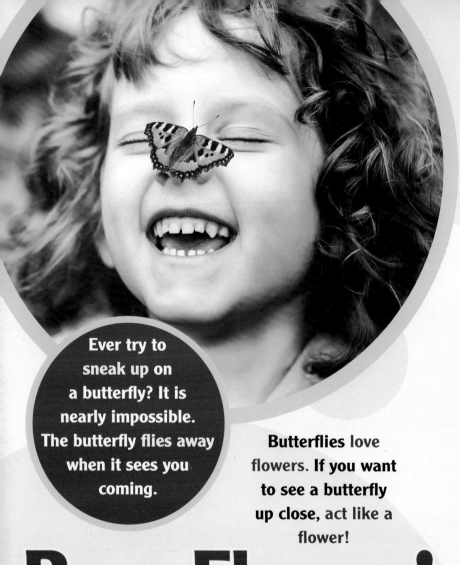

Ever try to sneak up on a butterfly? It is nearly impossible. The butterfly flies away when it sees you coming.

Butterflies love flowers. If you want to see a butterfly up close, act like a flower!

Be a Flower!

Wear bright clothes. A butterfly's favourite colors are red, purple, pink, orange and yellow.

Smell sweet. Butterflies find flowers by smelling them. If you smell like a flower, a butterfly might come to you.

Be still. Butterflies stay away from moving objects. If you stay still, they are more likely to come closer.

The Publisher: KidsWorld Books

Library and Archives Canada Cataloguing in Publication

Einstein, Wendy,author
    Butterflies / Wendy Einstein & Einstein Sisters.

ISBN 978-1-988183-46-6 (softcover)

    1. Butterflies—Juvenile literature. I. Einstein Sisters, author. II. Title.

QL544.2.E45 2018   j595.78'9   C2017-906845-8

Cover Images: Front cover: From Thinkstock: Jasmina81; tracielouise.
Back cover: From Thinkstock: Rostislavv; Purestock; gjohnstonphoto.

Map: From Thinkstock: base map, Maxger, 51.

Photo credits: From Thinkstock: Ablestock, 36; AIFEATI, 15; AnneSorbes, 19; Ariadna126, 28; Beo88, 36; BilevishOlga, 37; bookguy, 54; CathyKeifer, 9, 30; Chimperil59, 42; Christophe Rolland, 25; cicloco, 49; ConstantinCornel, 5; crwpitman, 51; DuxX, 57; Emissary_Filmworks, 6; emkaplin, 52; ErikaMitchell, 33; FamVeld, 63; floridastock, 40; forrest9, 58; georgewinstonelee, 48; gjohnstonphoto, 21; gnmira, 7; HeitiPaves, 39; Ian_Redding, 16; IMNATURE, 4; InViaion_ Photography, 14; Jag_cz, 8; Jan Rozehnal, 15; JHVEPhoto, 53; JillianCain, 28; Johnnieshin, 24; johnrandallalves, 38; Kagenmi, 43; Kaido Karner, 21; Katrina Brown, 45; LagunaticPhoto, 27; leekris, 40; lenta, 10; Leoba, 44; LeoMercon, 18; Lightwriter1949, 32; MargaretClavell, 17; MarkMirror, 35; Mathisa_s, 30, 34; mattiaATH, 33; michael Meijer, 3; michaelramsdell1967, 59; monkeystock, 46; nanoya, 35; NexTser, 50; Norbert Lochner, 39; numismarty, 42; oksix, 61; PapaBear, 60; Pedarilhos, 56; photosbyjim, 33; Purestock, 2, 11, 13, 23, 47; Rabbitti, 12; rainbow-7, 32; redtailcat, 16; reisegraf, 41; Rostislavv, 13; Sander Meertins, 26; Tadulia, 43; tahir_ abbas, 33; tenra, 31; teptong, 29; tzooka, 5; ulkas, 62; vmenshov, 7; wild17, 13, 55; WTolenaars, 22; yhelfman, 20. From Wikipedia: D. Gordon E. Robertson, 17.

We acknowledge the financial support of the Government of Canada.
Nous reconnaissons l'appui financier du gouvernement du Canada.

Funded by the Government of Canada
Financé par le gouvernement du Canada | Canadä

PC: 38